Blackberry Pudding

Written by Leonie Bennett
Illustrated by Julie Park

Sam went to Nan and Grandpa's house.

Nan made some tea and
Sam helped.

Nan made a bonfire and
Sam helped.

Then Nan wanted to make
a blackberry pudding.
'You can help me pick
some blackberries,' she said to Sam.

Sam and Nan went out.

Sam saw a tractor.
The farmer waved to him.

Sam and Nan went over a wall.

'I can see some blackberries!'
cried Sam.

Nan picked lots of blackberries.

Sam picked lots of blackberries.

Then they went back over the wall ...

but Nan fell over!

'Oooooh!' she cried.
'Can you help me, Sam?'

Sam helped her to get up.
'I can't walk!' said Nan.

Then Sam saw the tractor.
He waved to the farmer.
'Stop!' he cried.

The farmer took Sam and Nan home.

Grandpa helped Nan to get down.
'You can make some tea for
me now!' she said.

Grandpa made some tea.
He made a fire.

Then Sam and Grandpa made
the blackberry pudding ...
and Nan helped!